The Finite Infinite Frame: A

Angelo Chavez

BookLeaf Publishing

India | USA | UK

Presentation by *BookLeaf Publishing*

Web: www.bookleafpub.com

E-mail: info@bookleafpub.com

ISBN: 9789363306851

First edition 2024

*Dedicated to the person who was the closest
thing to a mother I ever had wether she knew it
or not - Crissy*

PREFACE

Is the world made for everyone? Or just for those who are willing to sacrifice their presence of mind for superficial pursuits of blissful ignorance?

Presence Eterni

Nothing to live for, and nothing to live against.

Stranded within stagnant time, purgatorial rest.

All motion is the same, just lit in a different shade,

so it stays, true, none of all can fade.

Oh, too late

Delusioned was I that, paid were my evil debts,
in their wicked currencies of despair and regrets.
 How little did I know, what was owed, was to
bear the essence of suffering through the
experience of a charaded fate, the arrival to
happiness ;

oh, too late.

So now I say good morning to the last of my
days,

and know, fortunes fade with mystic lengths of
hollow pain.

Swim for presence

Eye cannot create the world around me, The
world around me creates I.

So wondering now how to swim within, the ebb
and flow
of torturous strokes of learning, and intermittent
breaths of
heavenly presence in existence.

Perpetual Sunrise

Best to take true views from sidelines,
Assimilate all beauty with right eyes,

 for we have no core,
without that which we adore,

and content are those who know life as perpetual
sunrise

Equanimity

5

I am confused.

Sanguine, scarred, and cognitively abused.

Socio puzzle piece, brought to spiritual knees.

If we're all the same,
Who is reprieved?

Kaleidoscopic

Seek and you shall see, variable rays of the sun.

All shades of the light which make-up what is
done.

Then you will know, all that is true,
Is contrasted by blue,

And still so, absent is impediment to blissful
recreation.

Q.B.O.

Do not be afraid to not know,

be afraid to Fear the unknown,

Fear the frames of mind that capture turmoil and sorrow,

Fear not capturing life in the net of existence,

Fear losing your part in life's choir,

And Fear losing contentment to desire,

Fear what must be feared to the extent of what you know,

But do not Fear to let go and not know,
So is the way to grow.

Illuminative Abyss

I have forgiven the unforgivable,

I've doled mercy to the merciless,

And have returned from the point of no return.

I know what it is like to be burdened by life,
And how truly blessed is the fact that dark
pressured culm,

Still can bear a diamonds light.

Systemic Nodus

I hold the unperceived weight of a thousand planets,

Yet I'm not the only one to do so.

I carry the regrets of a million mistakes,

and I am not the only one to ever have.

I bear the emptiness of a lifetime of wasted hours,

and I won't be the last.

But in the end,

 I will always be confined, in solitary within,

my irreplacable sentiment towards it all.

Forever Maybe, Maybe Forever

I don't believe there is an answer to life, only a question,

and that question can be answered correctly an infinite number of ways.

So long as the answer is only a possibility and not a certainty,

because maybe lasts forever, so long as forever remains as it always was, a maybe.

Amid Eternity

I was destined to love my love long before I met
her,

Because out of divinely dreadful necessity, I had
already fallen in love with danger as a child,

And she was the greatest dangerous beauty I
could have ever possibly encountered,

A bouquet of perfection adorned with a trillion
thorns,

An extravagant sunset eclipse with an ostensibly
indiscriminately blinding corona of beauty,

A wonderfully captivating and alluring flush of
vibrant, poisonous, artful color in a black &
white world,

An ethereally majestic beckoning mountain peak
of a sporadic volcano,

An inarticulatable soothing sirens song amidst a
vast desolate sea,

An exigent calling to a martyred fatal expedition
of purpose,

The Alpha and Omega to the purpose of my
soul,

Her existence, Her beauty, Her flaws, and My
love stand inexorably,

Amid Eternity.

S.F.S.

To quest for education is as to find self
flagellation,

And to find your eyes upon the skies is as to find
the depths disguise;

To not know is as to be wise,

So smiles can remain smiles without discovering
the necessity of tears as replies,

And all that lives can live without discovering
what it means to die,

For the forest of knowledge does not
discriminate on what it imparts,

From the extravagant jubilation found atop the
trees leaves; down to the unfathomable horrors
of the depths of the roots formed of twisted
black wooden hearts,

The only way to unearth, is to bring about deaths
birth.

So tread lightly if ; to know ; is the purpose of
your seeking search,

And heed heavily to the warning to be patient,

For grandly constructed fortitude is a
requirement,

To hold both,

Reverence for the good of God,

And sympathy for Satan.

What Matters

We have eyes,
Useless matters without any lights,
Still so, irrelevant, to actual sights.
Unable to perceive intrinsic lies,
And internal sighs.

Sight Divine

My soul has chains that burden my heart,
And my heart has chains that burden my soul,
The locks for my soul reside in my heart,
And the locks for my heart dwell in my soul,
Hitherto bound, the keys are yet to be found,
Although when caught by such drawing eyes,
I feel I know now, where the pair, divinely lies.

Memorialization of Profound Amity

I can remember astonishing glints of blinding
light from diamond eyes,
Beautiful sights of shattered angels amongst
pulverized skies,
Lives of lies, kintsugized, and held with
traumatized pride,
Tye dyed time endowed upon souls of blacks
and whites,
Cosmic rides for gravel bound beings, wherein
Translucently shadowed plights were revealed
by nights moonlights,
Resurrections of wills while still mirrored by all
that kills,
I can remember, how it feels to have emptiness
filled.

Contentment For The Searching Soul

Entranced by her ethereal muliebrity, I felt my
soul start to bud with longing for such a woman
to bless me with presence in love,
For her to grant me access to her nurturing
pollen as I devote my buzzing service to her
continued blossoming beauty,
Such as the flowers and the bees need one
another to exist,
I felt our souls inexorable from intertwining into
an astoundingly mystical and transcendental
ecosystem of love, as one,
And that filled me with contentment.
But I was wrong.

Reapers Sowed Time

How was Sowed the grim that must be reaped?
In wonder I wonder, where is the time that has
been keeped?
How can the mind think both shallow and deep?
Things that die, stay dead, inside, those that are
alive.
But are those alive, able to reflect, inside dead
eyes?
Is it death, or life, that takes my time?

Still Failing

How am I deteriorated, yet still not broken
apart?
How am I defeated, yet still in the war?
How am I dead to will, yet still surviving?
How am I unaware, yet still unable to let go?
How am I not progressing, yet still discovering?
How am I breathing, yet still not full of life?
How am I failed, and Yet still failing?

Quantumector

I am dissolving into all that surrounds me,

and absorbing it at the same time.

I am not a body,

I am a point of direction,

Both pushed and pulled into a singular point of consciousness that perpetually eminates emotions beyond control,

My only purpose is to be, and fight,

for the phenomenological presence that fulfills me.

Captain; No Crew

Castaway upon a sea without an end,
My broken ship becomes my only land,
Distant silhouettes of enemies and friends,
But my Hull bears to many cannon holes to
make my sails bend,
I spend my days drowning in salted waves,
And nights alone shivering on broken bows,
To build a new ship from old should be my goal,
But a canoe cannot make due against the
merciless blue,
And comrades and foes alike take no notice
from their sights of such pitiful pikes,
So to sacrifice my ship only brings a fate alike,
So why not sink as Captain Damaged,
At least I can signal smoke from a hollow cabin,
And those friends and foes shall know,
I still captain MY ship down below.

Robes Of Hay

I am only brawns and bronze ; forced to be from
infant dawns,

Those in silk have no mind for plights outside
their ilk,

So they fear me for the blood and dirt shall stain
their threads,

And judge so (fear)cely from their cotton beds,

That I can almost hear them from my birth cell
as they shout ; overhead,

I clasp my shield and sword, it seems you've
forgotten to cage the lions once again ; My lords,

Beast upon beast I slay until on golden manes I
lay,

But only ivory robes can take the stage of their
play ; and mine sowed of golden strands, only
look to be made of hay,

So sentenced to the colosseum is where I
remain.

www.ingramcontent.com/pod-product-compliance
Lightning Source LLC
LaVergne TN
LVHW010851200726

843508LV00012B/2855